Funniest Riddle Book in the World

by MORRIE GALLANT
ILLUSTRATED by
Sanford Hoffman

Sterling Publishing Co., Inc.
New York

Library of Congress Cataloging-in-Publication Data

Gallant, Morrie
    Funniest riddle book in the world / Morrie Gallant ; illustrated
by Sanford Hoffman
        p.   cm.
    Includes index.
    Summary: A collection of hundreds of riddles and jokes
arranged in such categories as: School Daze, Family Values, Crime
& Punishment, and Getting Personal.
    ISBN 0-8069-4882-5
    1. Riddles, Juvenile. [1. Riddles. 2. Jokes.] I. Title.
PN6371.5.G347 1996
818'.5402—dc20   95–42542
                                                       CIP
                                                        AC

10 9 8 7 6 5 4

Published by Sterling Publishing Company, Inc.
387 Park Avenue South, New York, N.Y. 10016
© 1996 by Morrie Gallant
Distributed in Canada by Sterling Publishing
c/o Canadian Manda Group, One Atlantic Avenue, Suite 105
Toronto, Ontario, Canada M6K 3E7
Distributed in Great Britain and Europe by Cassell PLC
Wellington House, 125 Strand, London WC2R 0BB, England
Distributed in Australia by Capricorn Link (Australia) Pty Ltd.
P.O. Box 6651, Baulkham Hills, Business Centre, NSW 2153,
    Australia
Manufactured in the United States of America

Sterling ISBN 0-8069-4882-5

Contents

1. STARTING FROM SCRATCH

What does one star say to another star when they meet?

"Glad to meteor."

What did Adam say when Eve fell off the roof?

"Eve's dropping (eavesdropping) again!"

Why did Eve want to move to New York?

She fell for the Big Apple.

What must we do before we can have our sins forgiven?

Sin.

What is the moral of the story about Jonah and the whale?

You can't keep a good man down.

Where did money start?

In Noah's ark. The duck had a bill, the lamb had four quarters, the frog had a greenback and the skunk a scent (cent).

Who designed Noah's ark?

An ark-itect.

Why was Noah's ark filled with fruit?

Everyone came in pairs (pears).

What did Noah do for people who couldn't get into the ark?
He gave them a rain check.

What did Noah do while spending time on the ark?
He fished, but he didn't catch much. He only had two worms.

If Atlas supported the world on his shoulders, who supported Atlas?
His wife.

What was the greatest accomplishment of the early Romans?
Talking Latin.

Why did Julius Caesar buy crayons?
He wanted to Mark Antony.

"All human beings are born free."
"Did you ever see the hospital bill?"

What has ten legs and drools?
Quintuplets.

What do you get between sunrise and sunset?
Sunburned.

How many days are there in a year?
  Seven. Monday, Tuesday, Wednesday,
  Thursday, Friday, Saturday and Sunday.

What is the best day of the week to sleep?
  Snooze-day.

Where did the Pilgrims land when they came to America?
  On their feet.

Why does history keep repeating itself?
  Because we weren't listening the first time.

Who succeeded the first President?
  The second one.

How can you be sure to start a fire with two sticks?
  Make sure one of them is a match.

What is the first thing an elephant does at the airport?
  Check his trunk.

2. FIT TO BE TIED

Where do old bowling balls end up?
In the gutter.

What did they call Count Dracula when he won
the boxing match?
The champ-ire.

What is a tennis player's favorite city?
Volley-wood.

"Are you a good juggler?"
*"Fair. I can throw the pins up, but I can't catch
them when they come down."*

"Your nose is running."
"I know—it needs the exercise."

"Do you exercise daily?"
"No, Daley can exercise himself."

How does a physicist exercise?
By pumping ion.

What kind of bell never rings?
A barbell.

Why is a marathoner a good student?
Because education pays off in the long run.

Why did the silly kid wear running shoes to bed?
He wanted to catch up on his sleep.

Why did the silly kid wear his running shoes to school?
He wanted to do some speed reading.

What is a runner's favorite subject in school?
Jog-raphy.

What is the difference between an exhausted runner and a burned out veterinarian?
One is dog tired and the other is tired of dogs.

What's the difference between a woman who paints her toenails and a woman runner?
One marks the toes and the other toes the mark.

Why do women paint their nails?
It's easier than wallpapering them.

Who won the race between the two balls of string?
They were tied.

Why was the pig thrown out of the football game?
He played dirty.

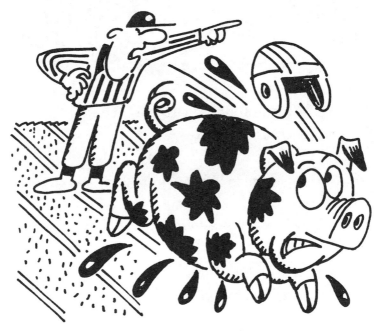

Where do religious kids practice sports?
In the pray-ground.

Why did the silly kid stand on his head?
His feet were tired.

Why wouldn't one foot talk to the other?
They were arch enemies.

When do the Siamese Twins go to a baseball game?
When there's a double-header.

"There's no place like home."
"Especially if you're on third base."

MANAGER: Remember the tips about pitching that I gave you yesterday?

PLAYER: I sure do.

MANAGER: Well, forget 'em. We just traded you.

How did the basketball court get wet?
  The players dribbled all over it.

What stories are told by basketball players?
  Tall tales.

What position would a ghoul play on a hockey team?
  Ghoul keeper.

"What would you do if a lion came after you at 60 miles an hour?"
  "I'd do 70."

What did one scale say to the other scale?
  "You have a weigh (way) about you."

What did the Boy Scout get for carrying a woman across the street?
  A hernia.

3. SCHOOL DAZE

Where do children learn their ABCs?
In LMN-tary school.

What's the difference between school and a
mental hospital?
*You have to show improvement to get out of the
hospital.*

FATHER: What did you learn in school today?
WILLIE: That four and four are nine.
FATHER: Four and four are eight.
WILLIE: Guess I didn't learn anything.

MOTHER: Freddie, why don't you want to go back to school?

FREDDIE: I can't read, I can't write, and my teacher won't let me talk.

"Why do I have to go to school, Dad?"
"Because I bought you a season's ticket."

"My school is so tough—"
"How tough is it?"
"My school is so tough, the school colors are black and blue."

TEACHER: Tommy, you try my patience.

TOMMY: No, Teacher, you better try mine. There's more of it.

"Here's my report card, Dad."
"Well, there's one thing in your favor, son. With these grades you couldn't possibly be cheating."

FATHER: You've got 4 Ds and a C on this report card.

WILLIE: Maybe I concentrated too much on one subject.

"Let me see your report card, Robert."
"Here it is, Mother, but don't show it to Dad. He's been helping me."

"Do you ever get straight As?"
"No, but I sometimes get crooked Bs."

TEACHER: This note from your father looks like
your handwriting.
WENDELL: Well, yes, he borrowed my pen.

"What was your favorite class so far?"
"The third grade. I spent two years there."

"I understand you go to an exclusive school."
*"Yes, the windows have bars on them so no one
can sneak in."*

"Would you children in the back of the room
stop passing notes?"
"We're not passing notes. We're playing cards."

TEACHER: What would you do, Sam, if you found
a million dollars?
SAM: If it belonged to a poor person, I'd give it
back.

"Are you in the top half of your class?"
*"No, I'm one of the students who make the top
half possible."*

TEACHER: I just caught you cheating, Sandy.
SANDY: Well, you don't have to brag about it.

TEACHER: Can't you retain anything in your head overnight?

HOMER: Sure, I've had this cold in my head for two days.

ART TEACHER: The picture of the horse is good, but where's the wagon?

BARNEY: The horse will draw that.

"Billy, why are you picking your nose in class?"
"My mother won't let me do it at home."

TEACHER: Tina, why are you reading the last pages of your history book first?

TINA: I want to know how it ends.

TEACHER: If you have five haystacks in one corner, five in another and two in another, and you put them all together, how many would you have?

HOWARD: One big haystack.

TEACHER: Does anyone know who broke the sound barrier?

BERNARD: I'm no squealer.

What do you call someone who squeals to the teacher?

A school (stool) pigeon.

TEACHER: Do you file your nails, Tommy?

TOMMY: No, I just throw them away.

TEACHER: Ronald, did you ever hear of the Golden Fleece?

RONALD: No, do they bite?

TEACHER: Eddie, stop your dreaming.

EDDIE: I wasn't dreaming. I was taking a nap.

TEACHER: What can we do to stop polluting our waters?

STANLEY: Stop taking baths.

4. WHAT'S EATING YOU?

What is a parrot's favorite food?
Macaw-roni.

What kind of food does a race horse eat?
Fast food.

What is a snake's favorite ice cream?
Hiss-tachio.

What's a snake's favorite vegetable?
Asp-aragus.

What kind of breakfast helps you play word games?
Scrabbled eggs.

What would you get if you crossed an egg with an ox?
An egg with double yokes (yolks).

What do Eskimos eat for breakfast?
Ice Krispies.

What does a gambler eat for breakfast?
Dice Krispies.

What does a comedian eat for breakfast?
Pun-cakes.

What is a comedian's favorite cereal?
Shredded wit.

What do golfers snack on?
Bread and putter (butter).

Why does the kangaroo carry bread in his pouch?
So he can have a pocket full of rye.

What did one loaf of bread say to the other loaf
of bread?
"I've got my rye (eye) on you."

How do you make an artichoke?
Strangle it.

How do you make a popover?
Do it right the first time.

How do you make a Yankee Doodle?
Give him a pencil.

How do you get milk from an elephant?
Open its refrigerator.

What did one refrigerator say to the other
refrigerator?
"Have an ice day."

DINER: What is that?
WAITER: That's a tomato surprise.
DINER: I don't see any tomato.
WAITER: That's the surprise.

Where did the homeless prune end up?
In the pits.

What did one prune say to the other?
"Do something about your wrinkles."

What can you pick in the garden that you can't
eat?
A guitar.

"If I had two sandwiches and you had two
sandwiches, what would we have?"
"Lunch."

"I think I'll fix lunch."
"I didn't know it was broken."

What is a caveman's
favorite lunch?
A club sandwich.

When is the best time to have lunch?
After breakfast.

Where does a snail eat?
In a slow food restaurant.

How does a carpenter eat?
He bolts his food.

How does a scuba diver eat?
He sinks (sings) for his supper.

What would you get if you crossed an Irish cook
with an Italian cook?
Stew-ghetti.

"Joe swallowed a dictionary."
"How's he doing?"
"I don't know. We can't get a word out of him."

What's the best day to have a stick of gum?
Chews-day.

What does a skunk do about kitchen odors?
It eats out.

What kind of coffee does a cow drink?
De calf (decaf).

What is a monkey's favorite drink?
Sars-gorilla.

What is a poet's favorite soda pop?
Lemon and rhyme.

What do policemen eat in Chinese restaurants?
Cop-suey.

"Did the Chinese waiter speak broken English?"
"No, broken China."

How does the butcher speak?
He talks turkey.

"Do you have any spare ribs?"
"No, I only have enough for myself."

How were the hamburgers taken to the police station?
In a patty wagon.

WAITER: We have fried liver, boiled tongue, stewed kidneys and pigs' feet.
DINER: Don't tell me your ailments. I came in for a chicken dinner.

"We're all out of goulash."
"That's stew (too) bad."

Where does sour cream come from?
Discontented cows.

What did one lifesaver say to the other lifesaver?
"You were mint (meant) for me."

"Did you ever see a salad dressing?"
"No, but I've seen a bacon strip."

What do you call a person who isn't allowed to eat chocolate?

Candy-capped.

DINER: Waiter, waiter, there's a fly in my soup!
WAITER: That's okay, there's enough there for both of you.

DINER: Is this onion or chicken soup?
WAITER: Can't you tell by the taste?
DINER: No.
WAITER: Then what difference does it make?

DINER: Are you sure this is chicken soup?
WAITER: Yes, sir. I picked a feather out of it when I was bringing it in.

What are witches' favorite desserts?
Ice cream crones.

DINER: Waiter, there's a fly in my ice cream.
WAITER: Let him freeze to death. It'll teach him a
lesson!

How do you make dough
rise?
Play the national anthem.

Why did the elephant dunk his
doughnut?
He lost his basketball.

How is life like a doughnut?
You are either in the dough or in the hole.

What dessert does the orchestra eat at
Christmas time?
Flute-cake (fruitcake).

What did Simple Simon say to the pieman?
"You've got a lot of crust."

What would you get if you crossed a wrestler
with a piece of pastry?
Grapple pie.

What did the cannibal eat when he went on a diet?

Only thin people.

What does a cannibal do between meals?

Burp.

"Is the fish fresh?"

"Yes, it nearly bit my finger off."

Can any birds devour fish?

Yes, the peli-can.

What did the oyster say as he was eaten by the minister?

"I always wanted to enter the clergy."

Is a clam ever generous?

No, it's always shell-fish.

What do astronauts do when they run out of food?

They go shopping.

5. TAKE TWO ASPIRINS

Why did the axe go to the doctor?
For a splitting headache.

Why did the horse go to the doctor?
For hay fever.

Why did the kangaroo go to the doctor?
Because he wasn't feeling jumpy.

"How do you know the teacher has a glass eye?"
"It came out in conversation."

What would you get if you crossed an elephant with a skin doctor?

A pachy-dermatologist.

Why did the elephant jump up and down?

He took his medicine and forgot to shake the bottle.

Why did the Chinese cook see his psychiatrist?

He was going off his wok-er.

Why did Chiquita Banana go to see a psychiatrist?

She had a banana split personality.

How did the fish get its nose fixed?

It went to a plastic sturgeon.

What would you call a doctor who has many investments?

A wheeler dealer healer.

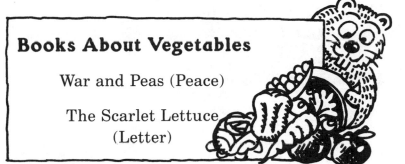

Books About Vegetables

War and Peas (Peace)

The Scarlet Lettuce (Letter)

"I'd like to change my doctor."

"He's a big boy. Let him do it himself."

What would you get if you crossed a doctor with a hyena?

A physician who laughs all the way to the bank.

What symptoms did the hot charcoal complain about?

Glowing pains.

What's the matter with the blackbird?

It has crowing pains.

What did one ball of twine say to the other ball of twine?

"I'm at the end of my rope."

What disease do witches suffer from?
Broom-atism.

Why did the clock get sick?
It was run down.

How does the King of the Jungle take his medicine?
Lion (lying) down.

What happened to the man who was sawed in half by the magician?
He hasn't been feeling himself.

"Do you believe in taking pills?"
"No, I'm anti-biotics."

"Doctor, doctor, I have a ringing in my ears! What should I do?"
"Get an unlisted number."

"I hear you had your eye tooth taken out."
"Yes, now I can't see what I'm talking about."

"How is your sore tooth?"
"It's driving me to extraction."

"Why don't you go to the ocean anymore?"
"My doctor told me to stay away from salt."

Why did the king go to the dentist?
To get his teeth crowned.

Why did the tree see the dentist?
To get a root canal.

What did the tree say when he saw the tree surgeon?
"Everybody wants to get into the axe (act)."

How come the man died when he was shot in the finger?
He was scratching his head at the time.

What's the difference between ammonia and pneumonia?
One comes in bottles, the other in chests.

Where does a rabbit go to have his eyes examined?
To a hop-tometrist.

Knock-Knock.
Who's there?
Oliver.
Oliver who?
Oliver sudden I feel sick.

"When you jumped down the stairs, did the ground break your fall?"
"No, it broke my leg."

What happened when the centipede broke all his feet?
He didn't have a leg to stand on.

"Did the doctor give you first aid?"
"No, I had to wait my turn."

"Were you long in the hospital?"
"No, I was the same size I am now."

"What are you taking for your cold?"
"Make me an offer."

What did the tailor take for his sore throat?
Cuff drops.

What does an elephant take for a running nose?
A case of Kleenex.

How do you prevent a summer cold?
Catch it in the winter.

What sickness can you catch from your mattress?
Spring fever.

Why did the fish go to the doctor?
It had a haddock (headache).

What does a snake take for a headache?
Asp-irin.

6. WORKING IT OUT

Where did the computer stay when he joined the Army?

At a data base.

What's the difference between a sailor and a jeweler?

One watches the sea and the other sees the watches.

What did the sailor say after he became a computer programmer?

"Don't give up the chip."

What would you get if you crossed a duck with a marksman?
A quack shot.

Why did the silly kid buy a thousand pickles?
He got a good dill.

"How do you know money talks?"
"Because I'm making every cent count."

How did the farmer fix his jeans?
With a cabbage patch.

What kind of button won't you find in a tailor shop?
A belly button.

What do you call a tailor who squeals on people?
A spool pigeon.

What is the difference between a tailor and a salesman?
A tailor deals in clothes and a salesman closes deals.

What's the difference between a man with a cold and a prizefighter?
One blows his nose and the other knows his blows.

What would you get if you crossed a baker with a prizefighter?
A bread box-er.

What would you get if you crossed a builder with a baker?
A house of seven bagels (gables).

What did the grouchy baker make?
Crab cakes.

Where do the best bakers live?
On the Yeast Coast.

"Why was your father's car recalled?"
"He stopped making payments on it."

What does an auto mechanic charge to fix a tire?
A flat rate.

How did the glass worker talk about his work?
He gave a blow-by-blow description.

What is the difference between a submarine and a plumbing supply house?
A submarine sinks ships and a plumbing supply house ships sinks.

How does a plumber feel as he finishes his job?
Flushed.

What happened to the worker at the fence factory?
He got the gate.

How far did the restaurant owner go in his education?
Through deli-mentary school.

What bird never goes to a barber?
A bald eagle.

"Why did you get rid of your watchdog?"
"It couldn't tell time."

What army officer works in the coal fields?
The major miner.

Which branch of the military does the most bragging?
The Boast Guard.

Where did the kitten get a job?
On a mews-paper.

If a dog bought a newspaper business, what would he be called?
A pup-lisher.

Why did the duck lose his job?
His company was down-sized.

Why did the trombone player go broke?
He let things slide.

What would you get if you crossed a
mathematician with a dentist?
A square root canal.

How do roofers march in a parade?
In shingle file.

How do roofers learn their business?
They start at the top.

What did the janitor do when he became the
boss?
He made sweeping changes.

What would you get if you crossed a comedian
with a termite?
A joker who brings down the house.

Why did the comedian give up his job?
He was getting jest (chest) pains.

Why does the shoe work seven days a week?
It's the sole support of its family.

How does a leopard examine his bank records?
He does a spot check.

Did you hear about the moon that was broke? It was down to its last quarter.

What stories do the ship captain's kids like to hear?
Ferry tales.

What's the difference between the captain of a ship and a soft-hearted judge?
One rules the waves and the other waives the rules.

Why was the locksmith so nervous?
He got all keyed up.

7. FAMILY VALUES

"Do you believe in heredity?"
"Sure, that's how I get all my money."

"What did you find when you traced your family tree?"
"Termites."

"If you're lost, tell us your name so that we can notify your family."
"My family knows my name."

What songs put baby birds to sleep?
Gull-abies.

Why did the deer's mother wake her daughter in the morning?

She wanted her doe to rise.

"Where's your brother?"

"Home, playing a duet. I finished first."

"If your brother gave you one dollar Monday and two dollars Tuesday, what would you have?"

"A heart attack."

"How many brothers do you have, Peter?"

"Four, but my sister has five."

"Did your baby brother finally stop crying?"

"Yes, my father gave him hush money."

"My father is a chain smoker."
"Mine only smokes cigarettes."

"My father plays the piano by ear. How about yours?"
"Mine fiddles with his moustache."

What does a skunk call his father's brother?
Skunkle.

"What would be the result if your father owed the grocer $400, the landlord $800, and the doctor $1,000?"
"We'd move."

"If your parents saved $50 a week for six weeks, what would they have?"
"A new TV set."

BETSY: Dad, where is the Taj Mahal?
FATHER: Ask your mother. She puts everything away.

MOTHER: There'll be no dessert tonight.
MORRIS: You mean I've been eating for nothing?

MOE: My brother, the magician, is going to saw me in half.
JOE: So then you'll be a half brother.

How did the hot dogs get married?
For better or wurst.

How did the telephones get married?
In a double ring ceremony.

What government agency finds lost ministers?
The Bureau of Missing Parsons.

What do bullets have when they get married?
Beebies.

What kind of car does Mickey Mouse's wife drive?
A Minnie-van.

How did the pebble's marriage end up?
On the rocks.

What did one tree say to the other tree?
"I pine fir yew."

What hog is married to several wives?
A pig-amist.

8. CRIME & PUNISHMENT

Why was the weeping willow punished?
For crying out loud.

"Does your parrot swear?"
"Only when she goes to court."

Why did they arrest the big cheese?
Its alibi was full of holes.

Why did the policeman give the dog a ticket?
For double barking.

Why was the actor arrested?
He stole the show.

Why was the barber arrested?
He had a brush with the law.

How did the gangster get caught?
He bought a new pair of shoes and they pinched him.

How did they catch the gangster who committed the robbery on Mount Everest?
He returned to the scene of the climb.

"Can you describe the man who embezzled the bank's money?"
"He was six feet tall and $5,000 short."

How did the strangler feel when he was arrested at the card game?
The choker was wild.

What kind of birds are most frequently found in captivity?
Jailbirds.

Why did the pencil end up in jail?
It was lead (led) astray?

Why didn't the crooked tailor go to jail?
He mended his ways.

"The town I live in is so small—"
"How small is it?"
"The town I live in is so small, the chief of police has an unlisted phone number."

What would you get if you crossed a homing pigeon with a serial killer?
A bird that keeps coming back to the scene of the crime.

What would you get if you crossed a serial killer and a waiter's best customer?
Jack the Tipper.

Fighting Mad

What happens when two surgeons fight?
Scar Wars.

Did the banana win the fight?
No, it was a split decision.

How did the clock get bitten?
By a tick.

"Is the octopus mad?"
"Yes, he's up in arms."

"Is the skunk mad?"
"Phew-rious."

"Why did you cry when your brother got beat up?"
"Because I'm my brother's weeper."

Fighting Mad

What small fish is always getting into fights?
The scar-dine.

How do mackerels fight?
They indulge in fish-ticuffs.

Did the insects have a fight?
Yes, it was a flea-for-all.

What has done the most to rouse the student body?
The alarm clock.

"Are you going to strike the match?"
"Only if it becomes violent."

How do trees fight?
They have a tree-for-all.

9. HIGHER EDUCATION

How did the giraffe do in school?
He got high honors.

TEACHER: Your shoes are on the wrong feet.
MITZI: These are the only feet I have.

TEACHER: What do you know about the Boston
Tea Party?
GEORGE: Nothing—I wasn't invited.

"Paul, can you name the three Rs?"
"Reading, writing, and recess."

What author is known for his very large vocabulary?

Webster.

"How did you like reading *20,000 Leagues Under the Sea*?"

"It was too deep for me."

"You should practice writing more clearly."

"I don't have to. I'm going to be a doctor."

"If I were to drop a quarter in this acid, would it dissolve?"

"No—if it would, you wouldn't drop it in."

What school game can you play by yourself?

Hookey.

"Why are you sleeping in class?"

"I've got to get some rest. I'm breaking in a new babysitter."

"The light from the sun travels at a speed of 186,000 miles per second. What do you think of that, Jimmy?"

"Big deal—it's all downhill."

"Can you name the Great Lakes?"

"I don't need to. They've already been named."

"I hope I didn't see you looking at Harold's paper, Jim."
"I hope you didn't either, Miss Stubbs."

"Are you an apt student?"
"Sure, I'm apt to flunk every exam I take."

TEACHER: Seymour, can you answer this question in Spanish?
SEYMOUR: I can't even answer it in English.

What is the swine's favorite subject in school?
Pig-onometry.

What is the moth's favorite subject in school?
Moth-ematics.

"Why do you call your dog Arithmetic?"
"He has a broken leg, so he puts down three and carries one."

What has a foot on each end and one in the middle?
A yardstick.

What's the difference betwen one yard and two yards?
A fence.

What contest did the skunk win in school?
The smelling bee.

"Can you help me find the lowest common denominator?"
"I didn't know it was lost."

TEACHER: I understand you just moved from Texas, Johnny. Did you have short division yet?

JOHNNY: No, ma'am. In Texas we only have long division.

TEACHER: When I was your age, Tommy, I could answer any question in arithmetic.

TOMMY: Yes, but you had a different teacher than I had.

"Why did you cheat on the test?"
"We weren't cheating. We were pooling our knowledge."

Did the India Rubber Man pass the test?
Yes, it was a snap.

When will the alphabet have 24 letters?
When U and I are gone.

"Does your father help you with your homework?"
"No, I get it wrong all by myself."

"Why are you running to school? Are you late?"
"No, it's on fire."

"If the school caught on fire, what would you do?"
"Throw in my books."

BERT: What are you doing with those art supplies?
GERT: I'm going to draw my own conclusions.

ROD: Do you know what they call the ruler of a Moslem country?
DODD: Sultanly I do.

What country has the largest population of male deer?
Stag-nation.

"What can you tell us about the Dead Sea?"
"I didn't even know it was sick."

"Why did Nero fiddle while Rome burned?"
"Because he left his saxophone home."

"Did you get any bad marks at school today?"
"Yes, but they are where they don't show."

Why did the silly kid study in an airplane?
He wanted to get a higher education.

"How do you like school?"
"Closed."

"Myron, tell me about your study habits."
"I have a habit of not studying."

"You can't come to school at 10 o'clock. You should have been here at nine."
"Why? What happened then?"

"It wouldn't be right, son, if I helped you with your homework."
"But you could try, Dad."

"This is the fifth day this week you had to stay after school. What have you got to say for yourself?"
"Thank God it's Friday."

FATHER: How was your report card?
DEXTER: Okay, except for one subject. I was like Washington, Jefferson and Lincoln. I went down in history.

"I see you got another bad report card, son."
"A teacher's job is to teach. Why should I get the blame if she fails?"

"My report card went from Bs to Ds."
"How degrading!"

"What did you learn in school today?"
"That two and two are four. Yesterday I learned that one and three are four. I wonder what surprises tomorrow will bring."

Why did the college give the baby ghost a scholarship?

It wanted the school to have a little spirit.

How did the thermometer graduate from college?

By degrees.

What did the hen study in college?

Egg-onomics.

What did one cannibal say to the other cannibal at the college reunion?

"How did you like the grads-u-ate?"

What word is always spelled incorrectly?

Incorrectly.

What do you get if you cross a termite with a book?

An insect that eats its own words.

TEACHER: You have ten fingers. If you had three less, what would you have?

DORA: No piano lessons.

What is a music teacher noted for?

Sound advice.

When are teachers well liked?

When they have lots of class.

What do students do when they come home from barber school?

Their comb work.

What do dogs do once they're through with Obedience School?

Go for their masters.

10. GETTING PERSONAL

"My voice is changing."
"Well, draw the blinds!"

"Why didn't you draw the blinds?"
"I didn't have any crayons."

"Are you still throwing tantrums?"
"No, I've got a sore arm."

"Why don't you hold your tongue?"
"My hands are full."

"Do you believe in letting sleeping dogs lie?"
  "No, they should tell the truth."

"Why are you combing your hair?"
  "I always brush after eating."

"What did you do after Joe gave you the hot
foot?"
  "I gave him the cold shoulder."

"Why is your head in the clouds?"
  "I don't want to get sunburned."

"Do you walk in your sleep?"
  "No, I call a cab."

"I sat on a tack today."
  "Did you get the point?"

"What would you do if you were in my shoes?"
  "Shine them."

What's good for biting your nails?
  Sharp teeth.

What one thing can you do better than anyone else?
  Be yourself.

What did one match say to the other match?
  "I'm burned out."

Why didn't the man want to be cremated?
  He didn't want to make an ash out of himself.

What kind of soap does a skunk use to wash his hair?
  Sham-pew.

"Do you know Beethoven's Ninth?"
  "No, was it a boy or a girl?"

"I was brought up on Bach, Beethoven and Brahms. What were you brought up on?"
  "Pablum."

"Can you carry a tune?"
  "No, I have a bad back."

How do you make a teddy bear (bare)?
  Remove his clothes.

"Did that man pick your pocket?"
  "No, it came with the suit."

"Do you keep your word?"
  "No, I don't have anything to put it in."

MOTHER: Did you do a good job washing your face?
LITTLE AUDREY: Yes, now I won't have to wash it for a week.

If you can keep your head when all about you are losing theirs . . . you'll be a head taller.

"I just bought a mirror very cheap. You ought to get one."
  "I'll look into it."

"Shall I cut the pie into six slices?"
 "No, I could never eat six slices. Cut it in four."

"Did you just pick your nose?"
 "No, I've had it all the time."

"What do you do when things get black?"
 "I send them to the laundry."

"Your face looks familiar."
 "Of course, I've always looked this way."

"Something is preying on my mind."
 "I didn't know you were religious."

"I boxed his ears."
 "Are you going to have them gift-wrapped?"

"What did you do when the bee stung you?"
 "Nothing, the dirty coward flew away."

11. IT'S FUN-DAMENTAL!

Why did the deer take the elephant to the party?
It was going stag.

Do deer enjoy themselves at parties?
Yes, they have a lot of faun.

Why didn't the hatchet go to the party?
It wasn't axed.

When do people who yell a lot celebrate?
On holler-days (holidays).

What is a soldier's favorite holiday?
Tanks-giving.

What did one ink spot say to the other ink spot?
"Come on in, the blotter (water) is fine."

What is the best day to ride in a boat?
Cruise-day.

What is the best day to tell jokes?
Pun-day.

What's the favorite day for fathers?
Dad-urday.

What starts out red and ends up black?
Santa Claus, going down a chimney.

What sickness did Santa get going down the chimney?
The flu (flue).

Why does Santa Claus travel at night?
The traffic is lighter.

What would you get if you crossed Kris Kringle with a bandage?
Santa Gauze.

What is a gardener's favorite game?
Follow the Weeder.

What is a cannibal's favorite game?
Swallow the Leader.

What is a tree's favorite game?
Follow the Cedar.

What happens when a bee joins a glee club?
A sting-along.

What is a ghost's favorite music?
Spirit-uals.

What is a fashion designer's favorite music?
Rag-time.

What is a termite's favorite instrument?
A wood-wind.

How do musicians march in a parade?
Tuba two.

What instrument can you play even if you can't
play music?
You can always blow your own horn.

What do monsters play at parties?
Hide and freak.

What do snakes play at parties?
Hissing games.

What party game do kids play in Israel?
Kiss and Tel-Aviv.

What is a kangaroo's favorite indoor game?
Pocket pool.

What is the best timepiece to wear when you're playing cards?
A whist watch.

What do rabbits read?
The bunny (funny) papers.

Has your dog got any papers?
Only magazines.

What magazine does a clock read?
Time.

What is a viper's favorite author?
Snake-speare.

What did the silly card player do with the scissors?
He cut the deck.

What do artists do on their day off?
They take it easel.

What kind of shooting can you do without a
camera or a gun?
Para-chuting.

"Did you enjoy the parachute jump?"
"Yes, right down to the last drop."

What kind of show did the clock have on TV?
A tock (talk) show.

How do hot dog contests come out?
Weiner take all.

How do kittens shop?
From cat-alogues.

How do you honor a chestnut?
Give it a roast.

What is a zombie's favorite day?
Moan-day.

What is a large bird's favorite movie?
"The Wizard of Oz-strich."

12. TOTALLY NUTS

Why doesn't your parrot say what you tell him to?

He believes in freedom of screech.

What does a parrot do with a pencil?

Polly doodles all the day.

What makes ducks so rude?

They always talk down to you.

What did one goofy bird say to the other?

"I want to be a-loon".

What animals are the most reckless gamblers?
Cows. They play for big steaks (stakes).

What do you call a story about a cow that has a fairy godmother?
A dairy tale.

What did the cow say to her boyfriend?
"Stop trying to pull the bull over my eyes."

On what side of the bed does a cow sleep?
The udder side.

How do you warm up a room after it's been painted?
Give it a second coat.

What did one watch say to the other watch?
"Got a minute?"

How does an India Rubber Man travel?
In a stretch limo.

Why did the elephant go to the locksmith?
To have his trunk opened.

Is the skunk very talkative?
No, he's a creature of pew (few) words.

"Do you use elbow grease when you shine your shoes?"
"No, I use shoe polish."

What did one sink say to the other sink?
"What's on tap for today?"

"Did you take out the garbage?"
"No, it already had a date."

How do bees travel?
By buzz (bus).

What people would never join a nudist camp?
Pickpockets.

What side of a house gets the most rain?
The outside.

LOU: How come you flunked out of Barber
College? Didn't you like cutting hair?
SUE: No, I liked cutting class.

"My alarm clock went off at six this morning."
"Did it ever come back?"

What did one ball of twine say to the other ball
of twine?
"Stop stringing me along!"

How does the Abominable Snowman pay its bills?
With cold cash.

Why is the zombie always broke?
Because a ghoul (fool)and its money are soon parted.

What did one shoelace say to the other shoelace?
"This is knot (not) my day."

What did one blackbird say to the other blackbird?
"Crow up!"

How did the crow cross the river?
In a crow boat.

How did the gnu cross the river?
In a ca-gnu.

Why is that cat barking?
He's learning a second language.

How do you make a weather vane?
Keep giving it compliments.

Why was the broom late?
It overswept.

Why did the elephant grow a beard?
He got tired of cutting himself shaving.

How does a European mountain call for assistance?

"Alp, alp!"

Who was the smallest man in history?

The soldier who went to sleep on his watch.

What do you call a talkative monkey?

A blaboon.

What do you call a fussy cat?

Purr-ticular.

What would you get if you crossed an ear with a steam shovel?

A part of the body that picks up a lot of dirt.

"Can you carry a tune?"

"Only simple ones. I'm not supposed to lift anything heavy."

"What's your name?"

"I don't know. I'm not myself at the moment."

"Is it true that you always answer one question with another?"

"Who told you that?"

TEACHER: You should put your hand over your mouth when you yawn.

RODNEY: What? And get bit?

What do you call a person with many belts?
Strap happy.

"If you're writing a letter to yourself, why are you mailing it?"
"I want to make sure I get it."

What did one lamb say to the other lamb?
"Talk is sheep."

How does the Liberty Bell know it's cracked?
Because it was tolled.

"My new house is flawless."
"Then what do you stand on?"

"Did you drive the nails in?"
"No, I only have a learner's permit."

"How do you make a footprint?"
"Give it a pencil."

"Did you make your bed?"
"No, I bought it."

How did the dinosaur file its nails?
Alphabetically.

Why did the silly dinosaur wear a baseball mitt?
He was hoping to catch a bus.

How do dinosaurs apologize?
They say, "I'm dino-saury."

"How did you feel when you lost your watch?"
"Timeless."

What do you call a person whose car has been repossessed?
A pedestrian.

What exam does an exterminator have to take?
A pest test.

What monkey works as a valet?
A flunky monkey.

How does a street organist like his job?
It's a grind.

How do acrobats fall in love?
Head over heels.

"Do you know the time?"
"No, we haven't been introduced yet."

What kind of hair do oceans have?
Wavy.

Why don't ducks grow up?
Because they grow down.

13. GRAB BAG

What happened to the crazy contortionist?
He turned himself in.

What is a skeleton?
A dead man with his insides out and his outside off.

What would happen if all birds of a feather flocked together?
You wouldn't need so much newspaper for the bottom of the cage.

What runs but never walks?
Water.

Knock-Knock.
  Who's there?
Water.
  Water who?
Water you know?

What would you get if you crossed a weeping willow with a nun?
  A sob sister.

What would you get if you crossed a weeping willow with a UFO?
  A crying saucer.

What did the skunk say when he went broke?
  "I'm down to my last scent (cent)."

What do you grow in your garden?
  A little older.

What is the least likely item to be found in the glove compartment of a car?
  A glove.

How do Siamese Twins express themselves?
  In double talk.

How do you make a sideburn?
  Put a match to it.

FLOP: I'm reading books on plants.
MOP: Botany?
FLOP: No, I got them at the library.

Why is a forest always congested?
Because trees a crowd.

What did one parallel line say to the other
parallel line?
"What a shame we'll never meet."

Why did the leopard go to the cleaners?
To have some spots removed.

How do you make a milk shake?
Give it a good scare.

How do you make a board walk?
Give it a pair of sneakers.

What is a reptile's favorite movie?
"The Lizard of Oz."

Does money talk?
If you give it speech lessons.

Why can't you trust a toreador?
He's used to throwing the bull.

"I like science when it's not over my head."
"That's the same way I feel about pigeons."

What would you get if you crossed a homing pigeon with a boomerang?
An Australian bird that never gets lost.

What would you get if you crossed a kookaburra with a comedian?
A bird that laughs at its own jokes.

What would you get if you crossed an elephant with a chicken?
The biggest coward in town.

What do bad little wolves become?
Big bad wolves.

Why did the bear go over the mountain?
He couldn't go under it.

What do you call an insect that talks a lot and then turns into a moth?
A chatter-pillar.

"Do you know much about gophers?"
"No, I don't know a gopher from a mole in the ground."

"What were you doing in the stable?"
"A little horsing around."

Why did the elephant wear pink suspenders?
It's color blind.

What should you do with a pink elephant?
Repaint it.

"I think you're a gambler."
"I bet you I'm not."

"Why are you backing into the house?"
"I was told to go out the same way I came in."

Why did the monster go to Iceland?
To ghoul (cool) down.

Where do pigs live?
In a high grime area.

What would you get if you crossed a pig and a pickle?
A dirty dill (deal).

RIP: When you go camping, do you pitch your tent?
PIP: Yes, but it doesn't go too far.

"Did you cut yourself?"
"No, it was a knife that did it."

How do you stop a chimney from smoking?
Take away its cigarettes.

How does a centipede buy shoes?
Wholesale.

Why did the dog wag his head and shake his tail?
He didn't know if he was coming or going.

How does a mixed-up cat feel?
Purr-plexed.

What did the woman say to the Boy Scout as he helped her board a bus?
"You're putting me on."

"How do you find the weather here?"
 "I hire a guide."

"Do you read Shakespeare's works?"
 "Yes, as soon as they come out."

What did Aesop's teacher say to him when he got to school late?
 What fable are you going to tell me today?

How does the goat keep his hands warm?
 He has kid gloves.

How did the horse dig a hole?
 Bit by bit.

How do you make a turtleneck?
 Get him a girlfriend.

When are two heads better than one?
 When you're selling wigs.

What did one dresser say to the other?
 "There's something I want to get off my chest."

What's the best way to tell people they have bad breath?
 By telephone.

"I'd like to know how long couples should be engaged."
   "Same as short couples."

"What is your model plane doing in the closet?"
   "It's looking for a hanger (hangar)."

What's faster—heat or cold?
   Heat—you can always catch a cold.

"Answer the phone."
   "I haven't heard its question yet."

"Is Joe still flat on his back?"
   "No, he's back in his flat."

How do you make a sidewalk?
   Take away its car.

How do you stop a mouse from squeaking?
   Oil it.

Why aren't there people living on the moon?
   The cost of living would be sky high.

How do you stop a train from running?
   Call a strike.

14. BAFFLERS

What would you get if you crossed a clergyman with a baker?

Someone who ministers to his people's kneads (needs).

Why was the physicist fired from his job?

He had too many ions in the fire.

"How are things at your father's pants factory?"

"It's the slack season."

What did the gardener do when he got disgusted with his work?

He threw in the trowel (towel).

Why is a mole always in debt?
Because it's always burrowing.

What do you call an unlucky spaceman?
A lost-cause-monaut (cosmonaut).

What is the difference between a tennis umpire and a Congressman?
One rules the sets and the other sets the rules.

What is the difference between a model and a person who carries a picket sign?
One has a striking appearance, and the other appears to be striking.

What is the difference between a babysitter and a psychiatrist?
One minds the babies and the other babies the minds.

What would you get if you crossed a fortune teller with a shoemaker?
A psychic healer (heeler).

Where do wild young cows live?
In a calf-way house.

Where do people study volcanoes?
In the lava-tory.

Where do stupid people stay on a boat?
On the nincom-poop deck.

When is a ship not a she?
When it's a fellow-ship.

Where would Atilla the Hun be if he were still alive today?
Probably in a nursing home.

What do you get if you hold a viper up to a mirror?
A snake in the glass.

Does the snake's house have a cellar?
No, just a crawl space.

"Give an example of how heat expands things and cold contracts them."
"The days in summer are longer and the days in winter are shorter."

"Give an example of an indirect tax."
"A dog tax. Because the dog doesn't have to pay for it."

What day are college entrance exams usually held?
On SAT.

What did the cat say as it finished its milk?
"This is the last lap."

Index